WAY OF HARMONY

First published in 2017 by AJ Heath Publishing

www.ajheathphotography.com

Edited by Ed Griffiths

Proofread by Vicki Vrint

Designed by O'Leary & Cooper – olearyandcooper.co.uk

Book Production & Project Management by David Brimble – davidbrimble.com

Colour reproduction by DawkinsColour Ltd – dawkinscolour.co.uk

Printed and bound in Italy by Printer Trento – printertrento.it

The Forest Stewardship Council® (FSC) is an independent, not for profit,
non-government organisation established to support environmentally appropriate,
socially beneficial, and economically viable management of the world's forests.
This book is made with paper from responsible sources and meets
the eligibility requirements stipulated by the FSC

ISBN 978-1-9997475-0-3

1 3 5 7 9 10 8 6 4 2

A catalogue record of this book is available from the British Library

WAY OF HARMONY

Portraits from Bhutan

AJ Heath

ABOUT THE AUTHOR

AJ Heath is a British documentary photographer based in London. He has worked as a freelance photographer for the past eight years and has had work published by *The Times*, *The Guardian* and *Al Jazeera*, among others. In 2014, he gained a Master's degree in Photojournalism and Documentary Photography from the University of Arts London. He then spent the next 12 months living in the Himalayan Kingdom of Bhutan. This is his first solo photography book. A second book of photography documenting the effects of globalisation on the Kingdom, entitled *In Pursuit of Happiness*, will be available in 2018.

To Mum, Dad, Emma, Nico and my closest friends,
thank you for all your love and support through difficult times.

INTRODUCTION

I first learnt about Bhutan, the mystical land of the Thunder Dragon, as a young boy growing up on a small island in the Bahamas. My grandfather's business partner was a great friend of **Dasho** Lhendup (Lenny) Dorji, who was a member of the powerful aristocratic Dorji family and uncle to the fourth king of Bhutan. Lenny and his family were regular visitors to the island and, for formal occasions, would come dressed in their stunning traditional Bhutanese attire and Lenny would recount endless tales and ancient fables from his isolated homeland. Although I was living in a completely contrasting environment, hearing about this mountainous dragon kingdom hidden in the clouds sent my innocent imagination running wild. I knew one day I had to visit the country.

And so, when, in 2014, an opportunity arose for my fiancée to undertake a year's teaching placement at a private primary school in Bhutan's capital Thimphu, we accepted with little thought, and were soon flying over the imposing snow-capped Himalayas en route to Paro airport. The flight between Delhi and Paro was one of the most exhilarating flights I'd ever experienced. The aircraft passed over four of the five highest mountains in the world and we were treated to a spectacular flypast of Everest. Unfortunately, my fiancée was a nervous flier and was aware that Paro airport is regarded as one of the most dangerous in the world, with only a small handful of pilots qualified to land there.

Landlocked between India and China, Bhutan is sometimes called the 'Switzerland of Asia' because of its size, shape and location in the mountains. As our plane weaved its way through the surrounding 18,000ft mountain tops on its final descent into Paro, the flight added an additional feeling of anxiety and anticipation to what lay ahead. I was riding a wave of emotion; I'd recently got engaged, completed a Master's in Photojournalism and Documentary Photography and was off on a yearlong adventure into the relative unknown.

From the reading I'd done prior to our departure, I was conscious that Bhutan was frequently described as 'the last Shangri-La' and that its tourism slogan – 'happiness is a place' – had led many to believe that it was the happiest country in the world. I was aware that Bhutan was the last remaining Himalayan kingdom and that, until the 1970s, it had remained isolated from the outside world, in a self-conscious attempt to protect its national identity from the effects of globalisation.

I had seen many photographs depicting the country's unquestionable natural beauty and unrivalled cultural heritage and, from what I had read, I knew the government was steadfast in protecting both. In the 1980s, under the slogan of 'One Nation, One People', the government began a cultural unification project that established as law the **Driglam Namzha**, or Bhutan's national code of conduct. This cultural policy consisted of a series of laws which governed how citizens should dress in public and how they should behave in formal situations. It also regulated a number of cultural assets such as art and architecture. The dress code requirement of Driglam Namzha meant that Bhutan became the only nation in the world to enforce a dress code on both men and women. It banned the wearing of all clothing other than that of the ruling **Ngalops: gho** for men and **kira** for women. Violation of the law resulted in a week's imprisonment or a fine.

In the last decade or so, Bhutan has received a disproportionate amount of coverage from the international press relative to the country's size, not only because the fourth king abdicated the throne to his eldest son and ushered in a new era of democracy, but also because of its uncompromising pursuit of Gross National Happiness (GNH). Unlike the consumer-led metric of Gross Domestic Product, the health of Bhutan's economy is measured in terms of a Gross National Happiness

Index, which is intended to direct the people and the nation towards happiness. The Index provides an overview of performance across nine domains of GNH (psychological well-being, time used, community vitality, cultural diversity, ecological resilience, living standards, health, education and good governance) and is built from data taken from periodic surveys – in other words, censuses on national happiness. But GNH in Bhutan is distinctly different from the Western interpretation of 'happiness'. As the first elected Prime Minister of Bhutan explained,

'We know that true abiding happiness cannot exist while others suffer, and comes only from serving others, living in harmony with nature, and realizing our innate wisdom and the true and brilliant nature of our own minds.' [1]

And while there is no official definition of GNH, the following description seems to be the most widely used:

Gross National Happiness measures the quality of a country in a more holistic way (than GDP) and believes that the beneficial development of human society takes place when material and spiritual development occurs side by side to complement and reinforce each other. [2]

* * *

It was 15 January 2015 when I flew into the country. As I found my feet, I quickly became fearful that, as a documentary photographer, I had missed the 'decisive' moment and that Bhutan was no longer the 'last Shangri-La' that so many had described. Instead, I found a young democracy battling many of the same social issues we have come to expect from developing countries all over the world.

The recent influx of development had greatly improved living standards within the cities, accelerating the rural-urban migration and leaving many villages devoid of working age inhabitants. The capital Thimphu has gone through rapid expansion and development, and is reportedly growing at the rate of 7 to 10 per cent a year, making it one of the fastest growing cities in Southeast Asia. The wealth divide between the rich and the poor is far-reaching. About 12 per cent of the population still live below the poverty line and a third of the population suffers from a lack of food security. There has been a surge in both petty and violent crimes. The recent increase in non-biodegradable packaging has caused ancient pilgrim routes to be littered with rubbish, and the cities' drains and rivers are awash with garbage. Additionally, the country is suffering from high youth unemployment, alcohol and drug addiction among the young is a growing concern and, according to the World Health Organisation, Bhutan now has one of the highest suicide rates in the Asia Pacific region.[3]

The most unexpected revelation for me was the high volume of civil service bureaucracy and the controlling influence of the government over the people. The civil service in Bhutan is vast and swollen; there are around 26,000 civil servants for a population of only three-quarters of a million people and, at times, it felt like I was living within a police state. Whenever I travelled outside of the Thimphu Valley, I was required to gain a travel permit from the immigration office, which meant I needed a letter of consent from my employer, details of the purpose of my travel, the precise route and planned nightly stopovers. But these government policies were not just felt by the **chilips**. There were numerous restrictions which controlled aspects of everyday life for all Bhutanese citizens. It is illegal to sell or buy tobacco products in Bhutan (although you see people smoking everywhere), the sale of alcohol is prohibited every Tuesday ('dry Tuesday'), there are 'meat free' months to control the consumption of meat, and traditional dress has to be worn during business hours or whenever the national flag is flying.

The Bhutanese are extremely proud people who have a deep sense of belonging to their country and worship their kings in an almost godly fashion. There is a strong sense of community values and caring for one another, which I'm not sure I have experienced anywhere else in the world. They are reserved by nature, but incredibly hospitable and, to my Western mind, can seem unnecessarily polite and respectful. They also seemed noticeably naive about the modern world, which has quickly infiltrated their isolated kingdom, and many seemed ill-prepared to defend themselves against the pitfalls of a consumer culture. It was common to see men walking down the main street of Thimphu with bow and arrows in one hand and a 3G mobile phone in the other. On street corners, groups of high school students would practise the latest breakdancing moves which they had learnt from YouTube, while devoted Buddhists tiptoed around an infestation of caterpillars littered on the ground. And there was the morning ritual of seeing my next-door neighbour releasing live rats she'd caught the night before into the nearest storm drain, while rails of pork and yak meat dried on her porch in the Himalayan sun.

As Thimphu gradually became home, the most noticeable disharmony which appeared was the cultural and generational clash between the traditional Buddhist way of life and the modern world in which the millennial generation was now growing up. The older generations had been brought up in a deeply conservative society, where dissent and criticism were rare. I found them generally more willing to stick to the party line, and so their opinions and beliefs tended towards the uniform. Nowadays, the younger generations are facing a cultural identity crisis as they balance their cultural roots with global citizenship, and many are stuck in a cultural limbo, chasing Western and other Asian trends and lifestyles. Their aspirations and values contrast starkly with those of their parents and grandparents, but they lack confidence and seem unsure of their place in the modern world. However, thanks to social media, they now have a platform to voice their social and political concerns and to try to enforce change. While I was living in Thimphu, I taught a digital storytelling workshop to about 50 school leavers aged between 17 and 20. They all claimed that they very rarely read or watched the news. Nearly all had Facebook accounts from where they would get their news updates, and, worryingly, believed that everything on Facebook was factually accurate.

Yet there is a fledgling creative scene beginning to take hold in Thimphu where the youth is taking the initiative. On most nights, Mojo Park, a live music venue in the capital, showcases music by young Bhutanese rock bands performing cover versions of Western classics, there are poetry recitals at Junction bookstore, which is owned and run by a young Bhutanese woman, there are breakdancing (B-boy) competitions held at the clock tower and there have been a number of photography and art exhibitions hosted at various venues across the capital. There is even an annual literary festival hosted by Her Majesty the Royal Queen Mother **Ashi** Dorji Wangmo Wangchuck (one of the four wives of the fourth king of Bhutan).

The young are extremely creative and talented when given the opportunity, but often have to battle against generational prejudices of the older generations looking down on 'non-traditional' occupations. They also come up against strict censorship and red tape. A recent movie entitled *Hema Hema: Sing Me A Song While I Wait*, a Bhutanese film made entirely by a Bhutanese cast and crew that has gone on to be screened at many international festivals and won several awards, was banned from being shown in the country, due to 'the various religious masks used by the characters in the film, which is not in keeping with our own tradition and culture.'[4]

But the most apparent battle between the pre-modern Bhutan and the new globalised era was the visual clash of the clothing that people chose to wear on the streets of Thimphu. In recent years, Western clothing shops have sprung up throughout the capital, stacked full of fake brands due to Bhutan's proximity to India and China. Nike, Reebok, VANS, Obey, Boy... the clothes rails had suddenly given the native population a choice they had seldom had before. The dress code of Driglam Namzha has softened over the years and now national dress is only required during business hours or when visiting a government building, school, monastery or other formal institution. Many of the older generation still choose to follow it at all times, whereas most of the young Bhutanese now prefer to wear Western clothing. During the late 1990s, their fashion inspiration was taken from Bollywood and Hollywood films, but now, thanks to the internet, they have a far greater access to East Asian popular culture, so many display South Korean and Japanese fashion and hairstyles. Among the most common were the K-Pop gang, the hip-hop crew, the check shirt brigade and those sporting clothing emblazoned with the Union Jack or the Stars and Stripes. Strangely, superhero merchandise was also everywhere, in stark contrast to the uniformity of the national dress code. After generations of being forced to wear the gho and kira, here was an easy and quick way to show individualism, even if a lack of variety within the shops meant that some people ended up sporting identical outfits.

Additionally, in an attempt to be more individual, many of the young have tattoos: a 2012 survey done by a high school in Thimphu showed that 26.3 per cent – 259 out of 986 students – have tattoos on their body.[5] For religious reasons, tattoo parlours are banned from operating within Bhutan, as it is unbecoming of a Buddhist to pierce one's body and hurt oneself. Although several do allegedly operate on the black market in Thimphu, most people either have to go to an Indian border town such as Jaigoan or take the more common route of friends using unsterilised needles and watercolour paints.

In an attempt to document the visual clashes of old and new, I set up a simple outside photographic studio in the main square of Thimphu and tried to encourage as many members of the general public as possible to let me take their portrait. It was a lot more challenging than I expected. The Bhutanese are by nature very reserved people and they seemed wary of what I was trying to achieve and whether it was the correct thing to do. They were easily embarrassed, and it often took persuasion and direction to get the right shot. To my knowledge, this type of photography project had never been undertaken before in Bhutan, and I believe that this was the first time that some of my subjects had had their photograph taken. Additionally, an estimated 60 per cent of Bhutan's population is under the age of 30, so I found this skewed the balance of the project and led me to photograph substantially more young people.

Over the course of three weekends, I managed to photograph nearly 150 people and, in addition to having their portraits taken, I asked each subject for their personal details (name, age and occupation) followed by two very simple questions: what made them happy and what made them feel Bhutanese. Disastrously, the notebook that contained all this additional information was lost during my turbulent move back to the UK. To my mind, this loss rendered the project incomplete and therefore unusable. But in an attempt to resurrect the project, I reverted to social media to see if I could track down as many of the subjects as possible.

Bhutan was slow to advance into the digital age, with TV and the internet only introduced in 1999. However, there are now over 250,000 registered Bhutanese Facebook users – nearly 32 per cent of the entire population.[6] Furthermore, unlike their Western counterparts, it seems that social media users in Bhutan are far more likely to add people they have never previously met in person. As soon as I arrived in the country and started posting photographs to Instagram and Facebook, I became inundated with friend requests from Bhutanese people, old and young, whom I'd never previously met. I wanted to take advantage of this trend, so I uploaded all the portraits to a Facebook page called 'Bhutan Youth Photography Project' which I'd set up for an alternative project. The page had been up and running for about a year and a half and already had over 1,000 followers, so I asked people to share the album with their friends and to 'tag in' anyone they knew or recognised. I needed all the help I could get, as Bhutanese names, except for those of royal lineage, do not include a family name. Instead two traditional auspicious names are chosen at birth by the local **Lama**, (although it is becoming more common for parents to now choose the names). First names generally give no indication of whether the person is male or female and as there is a limited roster of acceptable names to choose from, many people inevitably share the same combination of first and second names, so that on Facebook, people have to create nicknames in order for their friends to be able to locate them.

I had a surprising response to my search. Within two months of posting the portraits to Facebook, over 9,000 people had viewed the album and I was communicating with about three quarters of my subjects. The Facebook conversations I started having about the project unexpectedly added additional depth to the portraits; and I came to realise that some of the dialogue had to be reproduced in this book. Although the national language of Bhutan

Dzongkha is a major subject, taught in all schools, English has taken precedence and is the principal language of education. Even so, 'text speak' and abbreviations are rife in all written work and there is a danger that young people are not fluent in any one language. The dialogue which follows is reproduced almost exactly as I received it, with only small edits made where necessary for clarity.

This book is a collection of favourite portraits from the project. Bringing it to publication has been a very personal and emotional journey and I hope it portrays a true and honest reflection of Bhutanese society in 2015 while giving an insight into a fledgling democracy as it battles against the pitfalls of globalisation. Bhutan is an incredibly special country and I feel extremely privileged and blessed to have been given the opportunity to call it home for a year. I met some truly wonderful people along the way and I'm very grateful to those who kindly shared their time and stories with me.

AJ Heath, London, May 2017

1 Karma Ura, Sabina Alkire, Tshoki Zangmo, *GNH and GNH Index, Centre for Bhutan Studies*. Available online at www.ophi.org.uk

2 *GNH and GNH Index*, as above

3 Based on 2011 WHO data, the suicide rate of Bhutan was 16.2 per 100,000 people

4 Bhutan InfoComm and Media Authority

5 'Popular tattoos at odds with school indiscipline policy', *Bhutan Observer*, 3 August 2012

6 Source: IWS (internetworldstats.com)

NOTES ON THE TEXT

Some names and personal details of the subjects have been provided by third parties in good faith but may contain inaccuracies.

The collages on pages 42–43, 68–69 and 96–97 are portraits of subjects whose identity could not be traced. The author would be delighted to hear from anyone who can further assist on these or any other unidentified portraits.

Only the first names of those photographed appear in this book for reasons of privacy.

Where the age of subjects is given, it indicates the age they turned in 2015, the year in which these portraits were taken.

The dialogue in this book has been reproduced almost exactly as it was received, with minor edits made for the sake of clarity.

GLOSSARY

Entries are highlighted in bold in the text on their first appearance on a page.

Ashi Lady

Chilip The Bhutanese slang word for foreigner.

Dasho Lord

Dharma In Buddhism, the state of things as they are; cosmic law and order. Also applied to the teachings of the Buddha.

Doma Also known as betel nut, it is an addictive mixture of areca nut, lime paste and betel leaf, which is deeply woven into the cultural landscape. About one third of the country's population chews it daily, including women, the elderly, monks, and the young. Red stains cover most streets and its users' teeth are usually covered in a red sticky residue.

Driglam Namzha The official behavioural and dress code of Bhutan that governs how citizens should dress in public and how they should behave in formal settings. It also regulates a number of cultural assets such as art and architecture.

Dzongkha The national language of Bhutan. The word *dzongkha* means 'the language of the district'.

Gho The male national dress: a long-sleeved, ankle-length robe hoisted to knee level and cinched tightly with a *kera*, or belt, so that it forms pleats in the back and a deep pocket at the belly.

GNH Gross National Happiness (see *Introduction*)

Kira The female national dress: a large rectangular cloth wrapped from ankle to bodice and belted at the waist; it is fastened at the shoulders and worn under a jacket.

La A term of respect, roughly equivalent to Sir or Madam.

Lama In Tibetan Buddism, a spiritual leader, applicable only to heads of monasteries or great teachers.

Momo In Tibetan cooking, a steamed dumpling filled with meat or vegetables, served with a hot chilli sauce.

Ngalop People of Tibetan origin who migrated to Bhutan in the late ninth century. They introduced Tibetan culture and Buddhism to Bhutan and comprise the dominant political and cultural elements in modern Bhutan. The Druk Gyalpo (King of Bhutan) and most of the government are Ngalop and **Driglam Namzha** is Ngalop in origin.

Tashi delek 'Good Luck', 'Blessings', 'Cheers', 'Welcome'

Ting momo Steamed buns, usually served with a curry stew or soup.

Tshechu Annual religious festivals. The word literally means 'the tenth day of the month'. Tshechu are celebrated widely throughout Bhutan in various *dzongs* (fortresses) and monasteries, to commemorate the deeds of the Great Saint Guru Rinpoche, in the form of well choreographed masked dances and traditional songs. They are a rich form of the oral history tradition where the Bhutanese pass on values, mythology and spiritual beliefs through the dance drama. They are grand events where entire communities come together to witness the religious dances, receive blessings and socialise.

DORJI, 64, shop owner

I'm trying to track down this man, do you know him?
I took this photograph in 2015 during the Thimphu **tshechu**.

Hi, he is my dad...

I've messaged your dad on FB,
but sadly he hasn't come back to me.

My dad cannot write English... lol

Can I ask you a few questions
for you to ask him on my behalf?

Sure...

What is his profession?

He is a businessman. He runs a
traditional garment shop.
One of the oldest shops in Bhutan.

What makes him happy?

He is always happy. As a Buddhist, there
is no reason to be sad but happy always.

So what makes him feel Bhutanese?

Following our ancient culture and tradition, being a good Buddhist,
helping others, not following material desires, respecting our Monarch
are some of the things which makes him feel Bhutanese and proud.

SONAM, monk

SANGAY, housewife

THINLEY, 42, miner

What makes you happy?

Single malt whiskey in the evenings.

What makes you feel Bhutanese?

I love my King. That makes me better Bhutanese.

DORJI, actor

Name unknown

TSHERING, 23, high school teacher

What makes you happy?

Who I am makes me happy, the family I belong to makes me happy. I have more friends in real life than on Facebook – that makes me happy.

What makes you feel Bhutanese?

My dress, my thoughts, my values make me Bhutanese. Talking with strangers in case they need help makes me Bhutanese. Smiling even if I don't know the stranger who passes by makes me Bhutanese... N m proud to be Bhutanese.

DEEP RAJ, 21, travel tour operator and part-time NGO worker

Hi there, Sorry to bother you but is this you in the photograph?

Yes **la**, its me.

What is your profession?

I'm a tour operator during the week and love working for an NGO at the weekends. I CAN'T SAY NO TO PEOPLE HELP. We clean Thimphu every Sunday. More than three years. Recently we started working for someone I can't name. Our team cleans around places, where owners of buildings gave cash, which we hand over to disability care center.

So what makes you feel Bhutanese?

The way I think makes me feel Bhutanese. Of course culture has a big influence in my life that makes me take pride in being Bhutanese. It's a little bit of everything as a package that makes me feel Bhutanese. Like food, dress, language, respect for one another. Huge faith in my king and religion.

Thank you so much for your time.
Best wishes and **tashi delek**.

Tashi delek and may Buddha bless you.

TENZIN, royal bodyguard

What makes you happy?

Being an RBG and protecting our royal family is a great honor and that makes me happy and proud.

TASHI, 23, waiter

What makes you happy?
I'm happy for what I'm doing and [to be] born as a
Bhutanese citizen with a lovely King.

What makes you feel Bhutanese?
Wearing our unique uniform, culture and traditions and religion.

SONAM, 19, nurse

What makes you happy?
To achieve my ambitions makes me happy.

What makes you feel Bhutanese?
The religion, culture and traditions I follow
make me feel Bhutanese.

SONAM, 21, student of Korean

What makes you happy?

Happiness comes to me when I see other people smile.
When I'm the reason behind them [winking emoji].

What makes you feel Bhutanese?

I feel Bhutanese as I am born in beautiful peaceful country called Bhutan. Bhutan, a beautiful and small country in Asia is known for its unique culture and breathtaking places, Bhutan is situated in the Himalayan mountains n peaceful... I feel Bhutanese.

AMAN, 23, architect

What does your uniform represent?

> My uniform represents peace and unity.
> We're volunteers known as De-sung, safekeeping
> our country as guardians of peace.

What makes you happy?

> Being with my family and friends makes me happy.

What makes you feel Bhutanese?

> Being able to preserve my nations culture
> and heritage in my own way and a broad
> sense of having responsibility towards
> my country makes me feel Bhutanese.

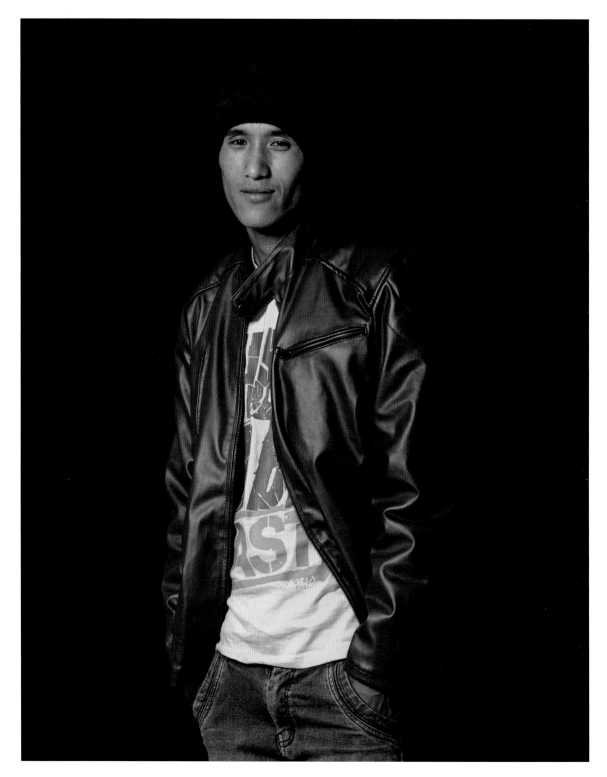

JAMPA

Name unknown

SONAM, 20, student in Class 11

Hi there, is this a member of Druk Jackson Boys
or do you know who it is? I need to track him down,
as I would love to send him a copy of this photograph,
but I also have a few questions I'd like to ask him.

Yes **la** its me the leader of Druk Jackson Boys and known as MJ la.

That's fantastic, do you mind if I ask you a few questions?
When I took this photograph in 2015, what did you do?

Yes la. I was a student. Studying at Pelkhil School in grade 11.

So what makes you happy?

That time I was proud when you click me picture.
Also when I dance and I inspire young youths of Bhutan
who are in drugs n alcohol, I just say to them that say yes
to dance n no to drugs. Till now I have changed more
than 70 dancers who were in drugs, that makes me happy la.

Wow, that's really impressive.
So what makes you feel Bhutanese?

Being Bhutanese is a great happiness to me
because Bhutan is most popular in **GNH** and I can see
peace and happiness in it. And our culture n tradition
are so unique and make me a strong Bhutanese citizen.

What do you do now?

Nothing, just coordinating my group everyday.
Inspiring them. Teaching them dance.

Good for you. Thank you for your time
and I wish you luck with your dance crew.

Thank you sir, means a lot.
Thank you so much for the picture la.

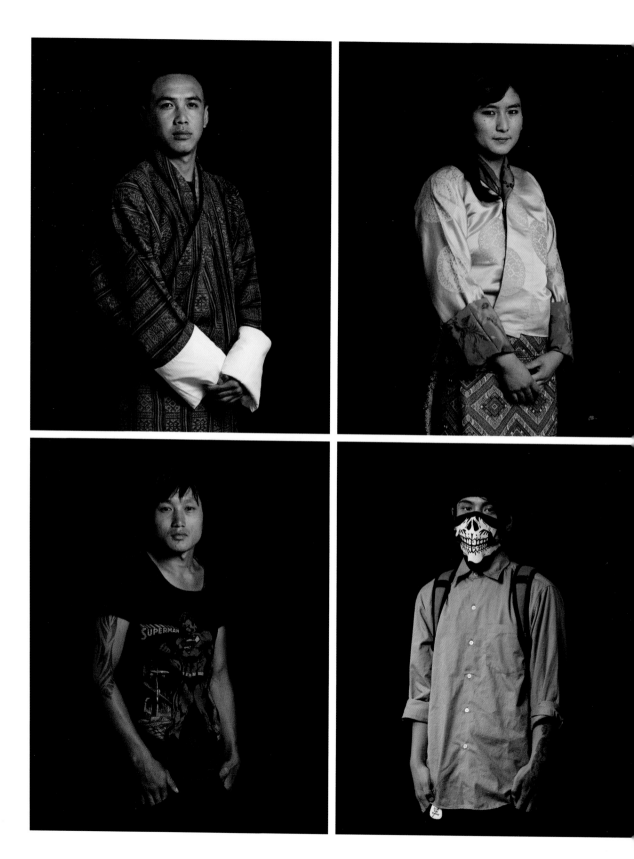

JAMYANG, monk

Name unknown, Hindu priest

TASHI, 22, college student of environmental studies

Hi Tashi, thank you for getting in touch.
Do you mind if I ask you a few questions?
When I took this photograph, what did you do?

> Yeah sure. I was at High School. Just dropped
> my college during that time [laughing emoji].

What were you studying at college?

> BA Eco. Environment la, but now I am a freelance model.

Two final questions.
What makes you happy?

> Modelling makes me happy. Whenever I'm down or
> whenever I'm stressful I always go for photoshoots
> or do the ramp walk [smiley emoji].

What makes you feel Bhutanese?

> The unique culture. Mostly our national dress
> makes me a proud Bhutanese [happy emoji].

Thank you so much for your time and
I wish you well with your modelling career.

> That's so sweet of you.
> Thank you [smiley emoji].

CHO, 23, student of business and human resource management

What makes you happy?

> My happiness is my parents and I normally feel good when I'm with my mom especially.

What makes you feel Bhutanese?

> I consider myself Bhutanese because I wear my national clothes, which is really unique from different countries all around. I speak **Dzongkha**, our national language and I behave well with people around and respect people a lot.

SONAM

MONICA, 18

TSHERING, 30, owner of a Bhutanese fast-food restaurant

Hi Namsey, thank you so much for tagging in Tshering. Do you know if she is on Facebook?

Hello **la**. Yes la she is my cousin but she doesn't have Facebook.

I have a few questions I would really like to ask her and would also like to send her a copy of her portrait.

Ok I will ask her and will let u know la.

Do you mind me asking what business is she in?

She runs a restaurant at Changjiji [a district in Thimphu].

Does she own it?

Yes.

Does she serve Bhutanese food or Western style food?

Fast food.

Do you mean Western style fast food? Pizza, burgers etc?

No la, like **ting momos, momos**, etc.

Delicious

Yes yes very much.
U wanna try it heheh...

Amazing Namsey, thank you so much for all your help with this. **Tashi delek**.

My pleasure la.

TSHERING, 18, student in Class 10

What makes you happy?
When I'm with my whole family and friends.

What makes you feel Bhutanese?
I feel proud about our culture and traditions.

THINLEY, 23, baker

What makes you feel Bhutanese?
My religion and helping mind make me Bhutanese...
Bhutaness we say [a colloquial word for the state of being Bhutanese].
Majority of Bhutanese are kind hearted and religious minded.
Moreover being born in Bhutan makes me a true Bhutanese.

PEMA, 23, unemployed

Hi Pema, is this you in the photograph?
Do you remember having it taken
back in 2015 near the clock tower?

Yes **la**... I do remember it la.

Thank you for coming back to me.
Can I ask you a few questions?
What do you do for a job?

I do nothing la. I had graduated
from vocational training institute.
Electrical la.

OK, so you've trained
to be an electrician?

Yup la, but there is no work for me.

What makes you happy?

Nothing.

Really? There's nothing that makes you happy?
Being with family, hanging out with friends,
your religion, partying, shopping, being in nature etc?

Nope.

Last question, what makes you feel Bhutanese?

Being Buddhist.

Ok, thank you so much for your time with this.
I really appreciate your time and for having your
photograph taken in the first place. **Tashi delek**.

Thnk u la.

JIMME, 20, student in Class 12

What makes you happy?
While eating CFC Gahah [the Bhutanese equivalent of KFC].
Helping my parents and to hang out with friends.

What makes you feel Bhutanese?
GNH... actually when I see people eating **doma**... hahaha [four smiley emoji].

TENZIN, high school student

What makes you happy?
Eating and hanging with my friends.

What makes you feel Bhutanese?
Wearing my Kira.

KELZANG, 25, civil servant

What makes you happy?

> Sir there are so many beautiful reasons to be happy n if I share abt myself I love being with good people... and the only thing that will make me happy is being happy with who I m...

What makes you feel Bhutanese?

> Sir m feeling proud to be Bhutanese... Bz we hv small boundaries covered with mountains with a glamorous environment... and all peoples r religious practicing **dharma**... So m lucky to be Bhutanese n m glad to be [smiley emoji].

Can you explain to me a bit more about dharma?

> It means people are getting more and more religious these days and they are practicing dharma visiting monasteries, offering feasts, donating and lighting butter lamps [a conspicuous feature of Buddhist temples and monasteries throughout Bhutan which traditionally burn clarified yak butter, but now often use vegetable oil or vanaspati ghee]. When one doesn't have a job, people think of getting enrolled in a monastic body and practicing dharma...

SONAM, 27, private finance worker

What makes you happy?

When I see little kids playing n smiling,
that makes me more happy.

What makes you feel Bhutanese?

Being happy and independent
makes me feel Bhutanese.

TSHERING, 17, student in Class 11

What makes you happy?
I feel happy when I overcome my fears and my wishes are fulfilled.

What makes you feel Bhutanese?
Our unique culture n traditions make me feel Bhutanese.

SONAM, 15, student in Class 10

What makes you happy?
Hahaha everything makes me happy.

JIGME, 23, unemployed

Hello, I believe that you might be related to Jigme
(in the attached photograph). Is this correct?

Thank you sir. M his younger sister Jurme and m really sorry for the delay since I wasn't able to go through messages since last few months. For your kind information he is in rehabilitation centre in Siliguri, India and its been three months n will be back only after 3 months from now. They are not allowed to use social media nor phones. So if sir want to know anything related to Jigme than u can contact me through this account.

I'm so sorry to hear this, is he ok?

Ya sir dnt worry he is ok. Just to get himself lil improve. **Lama** Shenphen Zangpo [a Buddhist monk from Wales, who has worked with youth and substance abusers in Bhutan for over seven years] has helped him to change.

When I took Jigme's picture in 2015, what did he do?

He was just an addict which he had been influenced by his frenz.

Was it drink or drugs, or both?

Ya both sir he take drug n drink too.

This might be difficult to answer, but I'm asking everyone I photographed two questions: what makes them happy and what makes them feel Bhutanese?

Being wit his nephew is his happiness, n that nephew is my son. N preserving our culture is what makes him Bhutanese, especially wearing his **gho**.

I really am so sorry to hear this news. I really hope he makes a full recovery. Please thank him for me and I really appreciate your time and help with this.

Sorry for delay. I'm out of Bhutan, so took some time to update Facebook. N recently I got good news from my family that Jigme is back in Thimphu from rehab n he has changed.

That's amazing news...! Would you mind if I were to use our conversation in my photography book?

No problem sir. N now he is very good. He has changed. There is no harm in saying some1 becoming good now. Jigme is back in Thimphu looking after my son, since m in Iraq working as a house help for an Arab family.

I'm so pleased to hear he's making a good recovery and hope he manages to stay clean. **Tashi delek** and thank you for all your help.

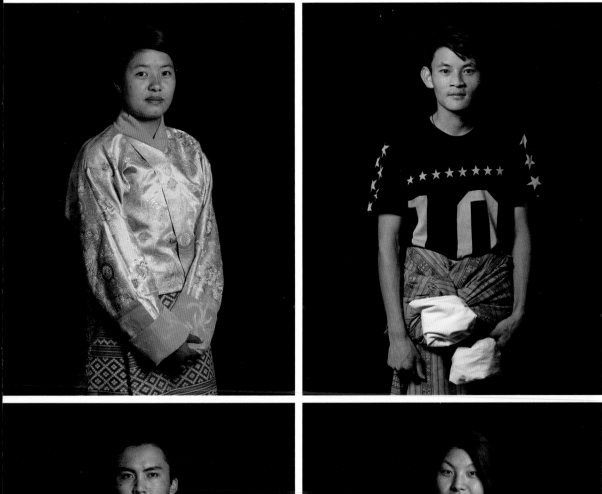

SUZAN, 16, student in Class 10

Hi Suzan, do you mind answering two questions?
What makes you happy and what makes you feel
Bhutanese? I really appreciate your help.

I'm sorry. I was very busy I forgot to answer you.
Yea I was in Class 10 back then, now I'm in 12.

Thank you for coming back to me. Can I ask what makes you happy?

Yea m thinking of it... give me a few secs...
if you don't mind can I ask you a question?

Of course you can.

Where are you from?

I'm from the UK and currently back living in London.

Ahh cool... Thank you so much.

I can't believe you were only 16 when I took
that photograph. You look a lot older than that.

Hahaha yeah I know... everyone says so... I am prettier now... hahaha...
just kidding. Being myself makes me Bhutanese, nationality is just a tag.

So you see yourself as a global citizen?

Yeah.

So lastly, what makes you happy?

Arrrhh that's tough... hahaha, there is a lot.

I know! Is it material things, religion, nature,
partying, singing, dancing, hanging out with your friends?

Painting

OK cool, what do you paint? What about painting
makes you happy? Is it the escapism or being creative?

Umm whatever comes in my mind, just simple painting on canvases.
Yea maybe being creative. And yeah hanging out with friends and shopping.
There is so many.

KHANDU, 18, unemployed

What makes you happy?

I like happy people and good vibes,
family, traveling, respect and helping
others, that makes me happy.

What makes you feel Bhutanese?

As a Bhutanese in Bhutan we have unique culture which attracts tourism
and I'm proud being Bhutanese. And also Bhutan is a peaceful country
where all Bhutanese get their own freedom. My inner instinct tells me that
our tradition, nature, culture and people are connected to one another.

TSHERING

TANDIN, 26

NIMA, 15, student in Class 9

What makes you happy?
Dancing with my all girl dance troop SSB – Six Sassy Bastards. My family and
friends makes me happy... actually I am very happy to be born in this country.

What makes you feel Bhutanese?
Beautiful Bhutanese tradition... **ghos** n **kira** etc.

PHURPA, 16, recovering from illness at home

What makes you happy?
When I fulfil my dream. My first dream is to get a job n helps to parents...
my second is to go to my dreamland... London.

What makes you feel Bhutanese?
The way we dress up n the way we respect n we follow our **GNH**.

HANNAH, 18, student in Class 11

I hope you don't mind my asking, but why are you called Hannah, as it isn't a traditional Bhutanese name?

> I don't know **la**. It's the name my parents kept.

Were you still at school when I took this photo?

> I was in 11ᵗʰ grade. I just finished my high school now. I'm on vacation.

Lucky you...! I hope you got the grades you were after. What do you want to do next?

> I'm hopeless for now because to be transparent my results were not good. My family doesn't have good financial background. I'll have to see. Can I understand what is the project all about?

Sure, I photographed about 150 people in 2015 when I was living in Thimphu, and I'm planning to produce a book with them all in. I'm trying to track everyone down, so that I can ask everyone the same questions. What makes you happy?

> Umm... there are lots of things that makes me happy. Actually I find happiness in happiness of others. [two smiley face emoji]. Who are you by the way? Can I add you in person?

Of course you can, my Facebook profile is AJ Heath. So what makes you feel Bhutanese?

> The things I'm adapted to. The environment, lifestyle, tradition, culture, people, food etc. But I feel to experience the other parts of the world would be of great pleasure and adventure. I'd be happy in that. Where are you from and what do you do?

I'm a documentary photographer from the UK, now back living in London.

> Wow nice. [smiley face emoji]

Hannah, thank you so much for all your help with this. I wish you well and **tashi delek**.

> You are welcome. Pleasure. If you come back to Bhutan do let me know. Would love to do more photography sessions [smiley face emoji].

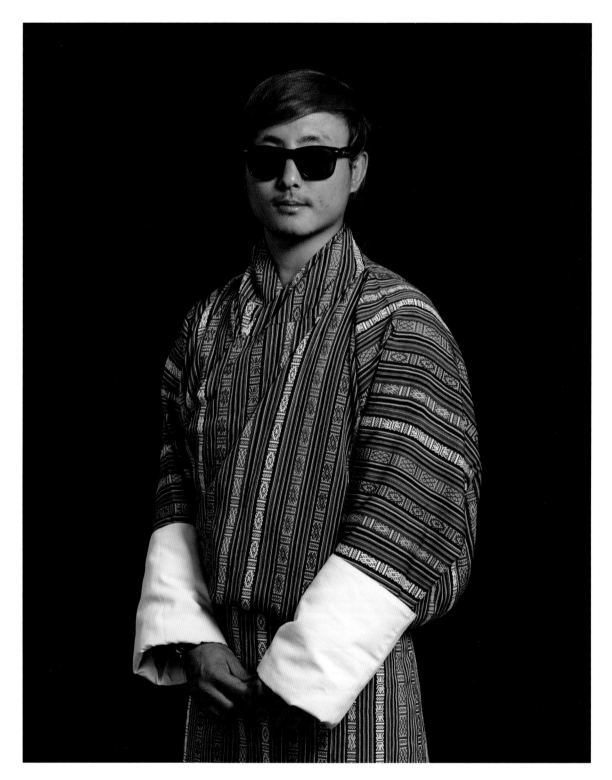

Name unknown

NAMGAY

KENZANG, 20, dancer in the Thimphu club

What makes you happy?
Dancing is my passion. That makes me happy plus making new friends **la**.

What makes you feel Bhutanese?
As I'm born under Buddhism I believe and it makes me feel Bhutanese.

KHANDO, 20, tour guide

What makes you happy?
When my wish comes true I feel so happy.

What makes you feel Bhutanese?
I am Buddhist and believe in God.

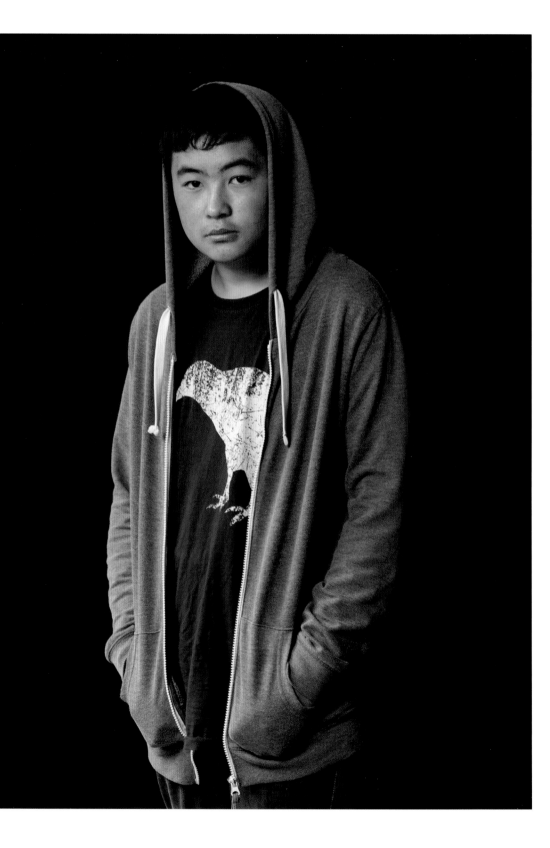

JIGME, 15, student in Class 9

What makes you happy?

Beatboxing makes me happy.

What makes you feel Bhutanese?

Wearing my **gho** and culture makes me feel Bhutanese.

TSHERING, 17, student in Class 11

What makes you happy?
When I can bring a smile on someone's face.

What makes you feel Bhutanese?
The language I speak and the way we dress.

KARMA, 17, student in Class 11

What makes you happy?
That's a hard question... I guess makeovers and shopping make me happy.

What makes you feel Bhutanese?
Our culture.

YOUNTEN, 19, student in Class 12

What makes you feel happy?

Self realisation

Can you elaborate on that a little?

Wen I accidently or unknowingly disrespect sum1 n
afterwards I realise wat I have done things tat I shudnt...
it gives me self pride n happiness cos m learning 4m
maself plus wen ppl teaches me n make me realize
d importance in life... It makes me happy.

Last question, what makes you feel Bhutanese?

My values and traditions.

Again, do you mind elaborating a little?

Values tat I have inherited 4m ma elders n
traditions tat ma locality taught me... it also represents d
culture tat I belong n the lifestyles tat I have nourished.

Thank you for all your time and for having
your photograph taken in the first place.

Its my pleasure to make u know me
and what I represent.

TSHEWANG, 21, unemployed

What makes you happy?
Playing football with my friends makes me happy.

What makes you feel Bhutanese?
I am proud being Bhutanese. It's a very peaceful country
and the people out there really respect each other.

SONAM, 17, student in Class 9

What makes you happy?
To me helping people makes me happy.

What makes you feel Bhutanese?
To me being Bhutanese is a very unique and proud thing so
I feel privileged to be able to wear our national dress.

SONAM, 17, student in Class 11

Hi Sonam, can I check if this is you in the photograph?
I took it back in 2015 during Thimphu **tshechu**.

Ya bruh... Y sir??

I took this photo in 2015 & I'm trying to track everyone down so that
I can send them a copy of the photograph. Plus I'd like to ask a
few questions. Can I ask what your name is?

My name is Sonam... U can call me apple...

Thanks Apple. So, what makes you happy?

Wen dancing feels me happi... [two smiley face emoji]

So what type of dancing? Do you ever do any traditional dancing?

I like dancin hiphop like other countries... n our culture songs...
traditional dncing lyk our rigsar n boedra sumtyms...
bt most of tym I like dancing hiphop... I even own a grup.

Can I ask you what rigsar n boedra sumtyms is?

Rigsar means like... the steps r like hiphop dnce...
onli the song is in dzo with beats... n boedra means like
slow a bit... but its steps in like waving our hands lik a wind

I presume dzo means **dzongkha**?

Ya

So who is your favourite hip-hop artist?

U mean grp?? Mmmmm... I like dancing like
jappawockeee n bradas... Dey be the best for me... haha

One final question: what makes you feel Bhutanese?

Mmmmmm... wen we follow n watch our cultural shows... [the tshechu
and masked dances which happen throughout the country]

Cool, thanks so much for your time.

Its ok sir... its my pleasure... ny help jst pls dnt hesitate
to ask me sir... hehe... thnk ku sir... means a lot.

KINGA, 12, high school student

DENCHEN, 14, high school student

BONING, 20, student in Class 10

What makes you happy?
Happiness is when I am with family and friends.

What makes you feel Bhutanese?
When I wear national dress.

PELDEN, 17, student in Class 11

What makes you happy?
My mom's smile makes me happy and when I dance too.

What makes you feel Bhutanese?
When I wear my traditional **gho**.

NGAWANG

I'm trying to track down this person. Do you know him?

> I kno him

Can you tell me his name
and is he on Facebook?

> Wait I hv to ask

OK, thank you so much.

> Hey really sry like I could not contact him. But I have
> told his friend to inform him. Really sry for delay.

Thank you for trying,
I would love to track him down

> I'll try ok. Like I have shared and
> have told my cousin to inform him.

Are you able to tell me his name?

> Ngawang

Thank you so much for your help.

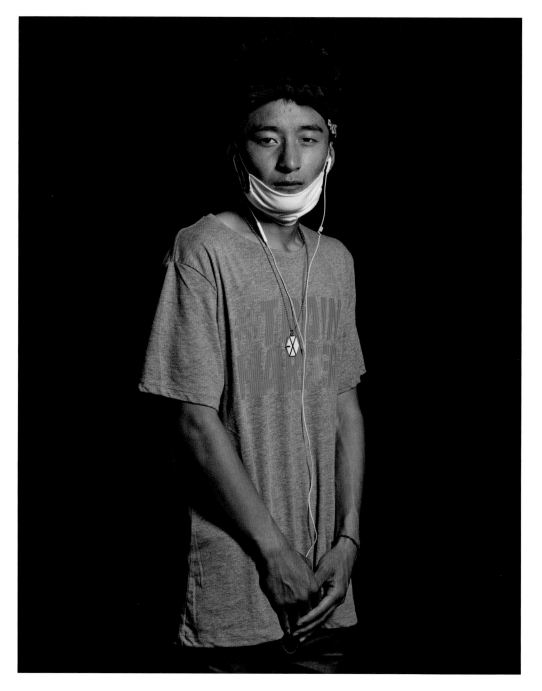

CHOK, 17, student in Class 11

What makes you happy?
Dancing makes me happy.

What makes you feel Bhutanese?
Being religious and happy makes me Bhutanese.

YESHI, 14, student in Class 8

What makes you happy?
Running in the beautiful Bhutanese landscape.

What makes you feel Bhutanese?
When I wear national dress.

SANGAY, 17, high school student

Hi Sangay, how are you? I'm sorry I've not been
able to send you this photograph before now.

Hello sir... yeah I do recognise you. How can I forget you...
you have clicked many pics of my dance crew
and I'm very happy and thankful for that.

Can I ask you what makes you happy?

Dancing with my crew, Druk Generation.

So what makes you feel Bhutanese?

Ummm... Basically our unique culture and tradition.
And yeah most importantly our religion.

Do you know anyone else in the album?
If so, do you mind tagging them in?

Yes I do know a few of them and will surely tag them...
there are only 3 or 4 peeps that are known to me.

Thank you, any help would be much appreciated.
I'm trying to track everyone down.

Thank you sir... We actually are very thankful that you have
done so much for my crew. Thank you for taking an interest in
us youths and for clicking pictures of my crew.

No problem and thank you for all
your help, you've been amazing.

Hope to see you in the future **la**. Goodnight sir.

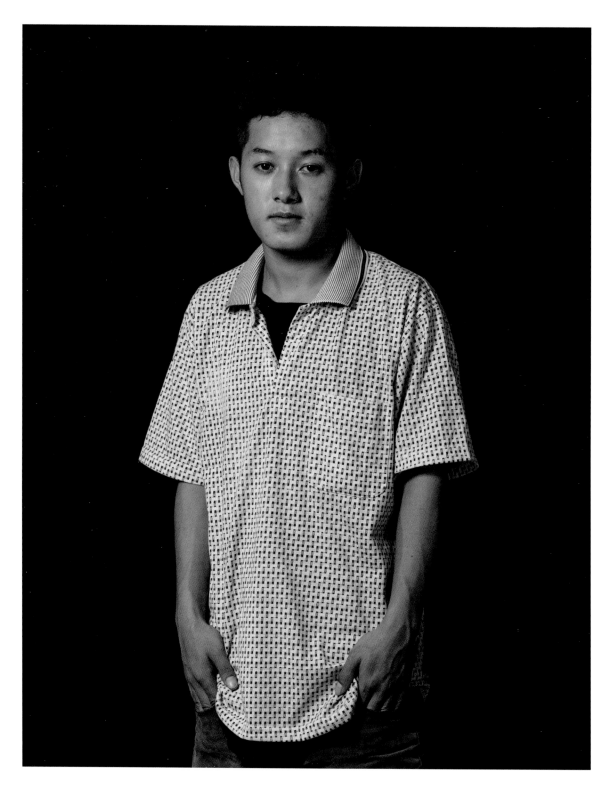

KAMA, 17, high school student

JAMYANG, 14, high school student

KELDEN, 17, student in Class 11

Is Kelden your first name or last name?

My first, its just Kelden.

Do you not have a last name?

No I don't.

What makes you happy?

Playing computer games. Dancing with my crew and hanging out with my friends.

What's your dance crew called and what type of dance do you do?

Our crew's name is 'Druk Generation' and we mostly do Urban Field.

OK, I photographed you guys a few times! Forgive me, but what is Urban Field?

Urban Field is a dancing style where you fuse dance with hip-hop, ghetto and all, mixing of all styles into one. It also shows some illusionary concept of dance.

So what's your favourite computer game?

Defence of the Ancient (DotA).

What makes you feel Bhutanese?

While I'm dancing. Although this type of dancing style is from the western part of the world. What makes me feel Bhutanese is that the crowd are satisfied with what we have to show and we are satisfied with all we give in dancing.

Does anything else make you feel Bhutanese?

A little of everything makes us happy. It's like when we're small the other children who have never worn a **gho** get to wear one so imagine the excitement and the feeling that the little kid would get? That's how I think I take things. Like everything is new so you get a lot of happiness when you experience it in real. But I don't know if I explained it right.

KUNZANG, 13, high school student

What makes you happy?
B-boying [breakdancing] in the park with my friends
makes me happy [smiley emoji].

CHODEN, 14, student in Class 8

What makes you happy?
Ya I m happy with m parents n frns [smiley emoji].

What makes you feel Bhutanese?
That its so peaceful n we r not under other country n people love each other.

SONAM, high school student

I'm trying to track down this person.
Do you know him?

> I know him, he's called Sonam. He studies at lzmss [Lungenzampa Middle Secondary School].

Thank you so much for this.
Do you know him well, as I would love to ask him a few questions?

> Yep I do but havent met him lately.

Do you know how I can get hold of him?

> Sry nope.

OK, not to worry. Hopefully he'll look at his Facebook account soon.
Thank you for all your help.

> Np [no problem] n best of luck [three peace sign emoji].

KINGA, primary school student

What makes you happy?
Getting good marks at school.

What makes you feel Bhutanese?
The food I eat makes me feel Bhutanese.

TSHERING, 12, primary school student

What makes you happy?
Playing games with my friends and eating pizza.

What makes you feel Bhutanese?
Having **GNH** makes me feel Bhutanese.

SONAM, 13, monk

What makes you happy?

I love listening to music, especially reggae.

What makes you feel Bhutanese?

Being a good Buddhist makes me a good Bhutanese.

Name unknown

Name unknown

JIGME, 12, primary school student

What makes you happy?

Studying.

What makes you feel Bhutanese?

Wearing my **gho** make me feel Bhutanese.

AFTERWORD

SANGAY, 21, photographer/videographer/sound technician

I first met Sangay during one of the digital storytelling workshops which I held in partnership with the Bhutanese Department of Information and Media and a local NGO called Youth Media Centre. He was a shy quiet boy, smartly dressed in a dark blue **gho**, with funky Korean-style hair swept across his face and a spiked earring through his left ear. He was one of the few students who attended the workshop who had obviously handled photographic equipment before, and was certainly the only one who came armed with a camera, which I later found out had been borrowed from a friend.

> 'I used my friends camera and till now I'm using my friends camera to shoot. Its hard to get for my own. I don't have any equipment till now... I'm planning to save money but it's hard to live here, so having a bad time with money.'

To begin with, he was particularly quiet and seemed to keep himself to himself. He was not keen to take part in group discussions and gave the impression that he was learning nothing new.

As the two-week workshop progressed, the students slowly started to come out of their shells. In Bhutan, they still use rote learning techniques in schools, so were not used to being asked questions or partaking in group discussions. They were all scared of answering questions (or even asking them) in case they were wrong or were made to look stupid. But I could tell Sangay was growing in confidence and really enjoying the experience. He was much more vocal in the classroom and I even saw him giving advice and helping out others. He was very keen to learn as much as he could and, unlike some of the other students, he knew he wanted a career in the film or photography industry. However, when it came to the final piece of coursework, a short multimedia piece, he chose to do it by himself rather than in the groups preferred by everyone else. His was certainly not the best within the group and it seemed he hadn't taken on board as much as I had hoped he would.

It was during these final projects that I started to grasp the extent of the drug problem facing the youth of Bhutan. Indeed, one group decided to do their multimedia project on drug addiction, which started an honest discussion where several students admitted to having a problem. Sangay was one of them. He openly admitted that he was a recovering addict, that he had started using drugs and alcohol when he was very young, but that he was now clean and determined to do something with his life.

I had been looking for an assistant/fixer/interpreter to help me with the various photography projects I had planned to undertake while in Bhutan. I offered Sangay the part-time role and he duly accepted. Over the course of the next five to six months, Sangay assisted me on various projects, including the portraiture project which makes up this book. We got to know each other well and I started to hear about his life before he was clean. He has had to deal with much more than most do in a lifetime, but my overriding feeling was how impressed I was with his drive and determination to turn his life around. The following conversation between us tells some of his story and is reproduced with his permission.

When you were younger and you were drinking
and taking drugs, what were you taking?

> I used to take hard drink like Black Mountain and Rock Bee
> [types of whiskey]. I used to sniff liquids and Fevicol, a type of
> glue to stick metals which is really dangerous on the brain.
> Many youths in Bhutan take tablets like RP, N10 and SP
> which are illegal and are imported from India.

What do these drugs do?
Do you know what the 'high' is like?

> RP & SP usually give high like as if we are in dreams
> and cool feeling but the N10 is very bad because it
> makes people wild... so most people take SP & RP.

Do people you know smoke hash and marijuana?

> Yeah these days people smoke hash and marijuana,
> even the girls do and there is many people I know.
> Sometimes I try to convince them not to do.

Please do not feel like you have to answer any
of these questions. Did you have to go to rehab
or were you able to get off them yourself?

> I didn't go because that time I don't have anyone
> to support me, so just left drugs all by myself.

That's amazing, what you've achieved is
really incredible. How old were you when
you started drinking and taking drugs?

> I started at the age of 8 to 9, was too young to start.

Who introduced you to them?

I started myself because of family problems. My late father was alcoholic too and he looked down on me because when I was in my mother's womb my parents got divorced so he don't look on me after they got back again.

Sangay, that's terrible, did he hit or abuse you?

The truth is that he hit me badly and tried to throw me in the river. He suicide himself at home when I was in Class 8. My mother is at [her] village with a new husband but I haven't seen her since I left home in the year 2013.

Sangay, I'm so sorry to hear this.
Are you sure you don't mind me using this in my book?
I can only imagine how painful this is for you.

It's okay, people should know about it. I would love you to mention that because I want to get people inspired from my story. I want people to know the difference being an alcoholic.

That is very true, but you should be very proud of yourself.
You've had to deal with way more stuff than most people
do in their lifetime and you've really turned your life around.
Good luck with the photo shoot on the 7th and
let me know how it goes.

I just want to thank you for giving me the opportunity to learn from you and I hope to work with you in the future.

Since I left Bhutan, we have stayed in touch through Facebook and Sangay has set up a Facebook page called Gyalgo Photography[†]. He regularly messages me to see what I'm up to but also to send me photographs he's recently taken. He is currently living in a shared flat with cousins and other family members and shares a room with his brother-in-law. He has just secured his first paid photography assignment with a Tibetan who lives in the USA. He is also paid for film work and worked as a sound operator for the film *Hema Hema: Sing Me A Song While I Wait*, which was banned in Bhutan but shown around the world (see *Introduction*).

He is a great example of what the younger generations can achieve, yet has also talked to me about his ongoing struggle to get his family to support his career and help to buy photographic equipment for him. He currently still borrows a camera from a friend.

[†]www.facebook.com/gyalgophotography/

FURTHER READING

BOOKS

Karma Phuntsho, *The History of Bhutan*. Penguin, 2016.

Madeline Drexler, *A Splendid Isolation: Lessons on Happiness from the Kingdom of Bhutan*. CreateSpace, 2014.

Linda Leaming, *A Field Guide to Happiness: What I Learned in Bhutan about Living, Loving and Waking Up*. Hay House, 2014.

Ashi Dorji Wangmo Wangchuck, *Treasures of the Thunder Dragon: A Portrait of Bhutan*. Viking India, 2012.

Serena Chopra, *Bhutan: A Certain Modernity*. Photoink, 2006. [Available from AbeBooks]

Matthieu Ricard, *Bhutan: The Land of Serenity*. Thames & Hudson, 2012.

ONLINE

Karma Ura, Sabina Alkire, Tshoki Zangmo, *GNH and GNH Index*. [Available online at ophi.org.uk]

Kinley Dorji, *Bhutan's Current Crisis: A View from Thimphu*. [Available as a pdf to download from repository.forcedmigration.org]

Foad Hamidi and Melanie Baljko, *Facebook use in Bhutan: A Comparative Study*. [Available as a pdf to download from researchgate.net]

Emma Varvaloucas, *Bhutan on the Brink: An interview with Dr. Karma Phuntsho*. [Published in *Tricycle Magazine* tricycle.org/magazine/]

Andrew Buncombe, *Is Bhutan the Happiest Place in the World?* [Published in the *Independent* independent.co.uk]

Every Culture: Bhutan. [Available at everyculture.com/A-Bo/Bhutan.html]

How social media woke up Bhutan. [Available at bbc.co.uk/news/world-asia-25314578]

Smita Pranav Kothari, *Bhutan: Now and Then*. [Available online from LinkedIn Pulse]

Karma Phuntsho, *Driglam Namzha: Bhutan's code of etiquette*. [Published on kuenselonline.com]

NEWSPAPERS AND JOURNALS

Kuensel Online kuenselonline.com
   The national newspaper of the Kingdom of Bhutan. It was the only local newspaper available in Bhutan until 2006 when two more newspapers were launched. The government of Bhutan owns 51% of Kuensel while 49% is held by the public.

Bhutan Observer bhutanobserver.bt

The Druk Journal drukjournal.bt
   Particularly useful articles in *The Druk Journal* include:
   What makes you not a Bhutanese?
   The Promise of Broken Youth: A Positive Perspective
   What is the 'Bhutanese-ness' of the Bhutanese people?
   The Nation, the State, the Nation-State: How do we talk about what we are?

NGOs

The Tarayana Foundation tarayanafoundation.org
Bhutan Youth Development Fund bhutanyouth.org
The Loden Foundation loden.org

ACKNOWLEDGEMENTS

It has taken me almost 10 years to get to the position of publishing my first solo photography book and there are far too many people to mention by name.

Starting out as a freelance photographer was a lonely experience so, from a photographic perspective, a special thank you must go to Chris Allerton. Not only have I learnt a huge amount through working with you but you have been a constant support and have always given great advice.

To those in Bhutan: a heartfelt thank you to Ashi Sonam Choden Dorji and Dasho Wangdi Jamyang for their incredible hospitality and generosity. Your home always felt like a home from home and, for that, I will be forever grateful. I am also deeply grateful to Dasho Paljor J (Benji) Dorji, Ashi Khendum Dorji, Kelly Dorji, Kinley T Wangchuk (former Director General of the Department of Information and Media), Karma Dorji and Thinley Dorji. I would also like to thank all my subjects for taking the time to have their portraits taken and for sharing their stories with me. And, of course, I have to mention Sangay Dorji for his hard work in assisting me with all the various photography projects whilst I was living in Bhutan.

The book itself has been an incredibly emotional journey and I would like to thank everyone who worked so hard to make it happen: in particular, to David Brimble for managing the project and for his expert skills with the image reproduction. To my brilliant editor Ed Griffiths for the tireless task of trawling through all the Facebook communications and for his helpful feedback and support with the written words. To Tara O'Leary and John Cooper for their creative skill in designing the book, in particular capturing the spirit of the Facebook conversations. Last but by no means least, to Vicki Vrint for proofreading the manuscript at its various stages.